ENDANGERED ⚠️

THIS ↑ ANIMAL GUIDE

BELONGS TO:

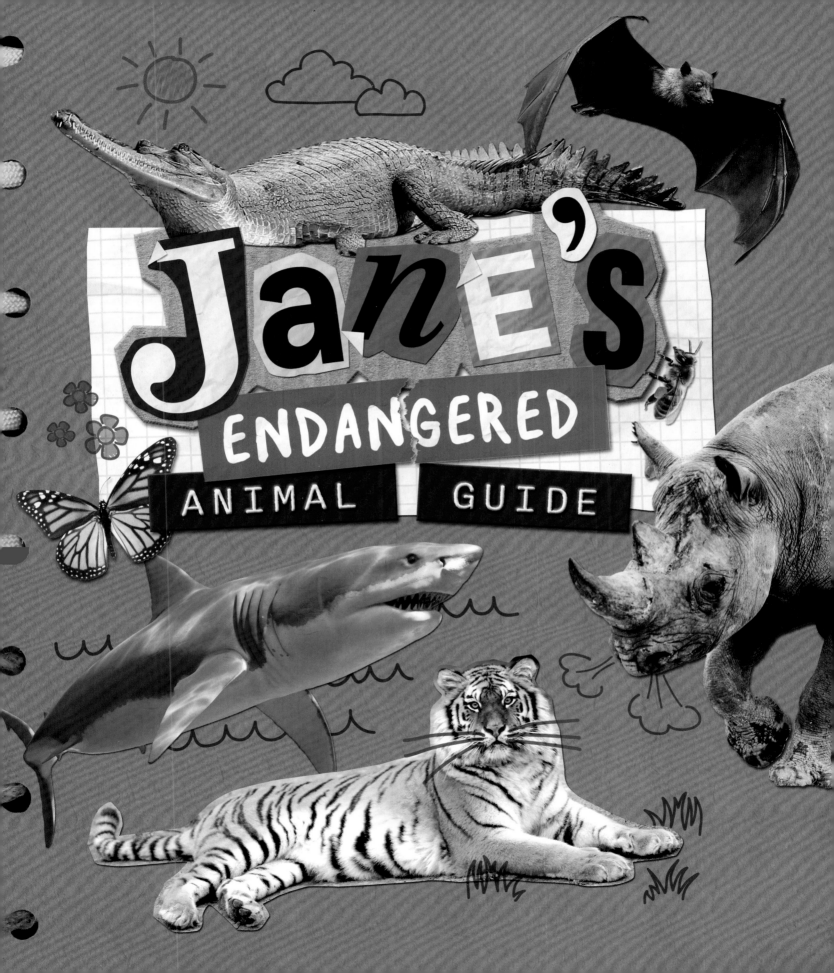

THAT'S ME!

GREYBEARD

DAVID

Jane's ENDANGERED ANIMAL GUIDE

J.J. Johnson & Christin Simms

Mango Publishing Group
2850 S Douglas Road, 2nd Floor
Coral Gables, FL 33134 USA
info@mango.bz

For special orders, quantity sales, course adoptions and corporate sales, please email the publisher at sales@mango.bz. For trade and wholesale sales, please contact Ingram Publisher Services at customer.service@ingramcontent.com or +1.800.509.4887.

Jane's Endangered Animal Guide
Library of Congress Cataloging-in-Publication number: 2022950389
ISBN: (print) 978-1-68481-177-9, (ebook) 978-1-68481-178-6
BISAC category code: JNF051100, JUVENILE NONFICTION / Science & Nature / Environmental Science & Ecosystems

Printed in China

POLAR BEAR MOM

POLAR BEAR
CUBS

ACKNOWLEDGMENTS

Matt Bishop, J.J. Johnson, Blair Powers, Partners, Sinking Ship Entertainment.

Kate Sanagan, Head of Sales and Distribution, Sinking Ship Entertainment.

Alexis Grieve, Director of Partnerships, Sinking Ship Entertainment.

Andria Teather, Senior Advisor, The Jane Goodall Institute.

Book Design by Francesca Willett.

Additional design by Amiel Lapuebla.

Special thanks to Margaret Smith, Daniel Rose, Teodora Ilie.

Extra Special Thanks to Dr. Jane Goodall for endless inspiration.

All CGI animal designs and artwork designed in house by the Emmy™ Award Winning Sinking Ship Entertainment VFX team.

DEDICATION

Jane Garcia loves Jane Goodall quotes and so do I!

One of my **FAVORITE** quotes from Dr. Goodall is:

"You cannot share your life with a dog or a cat and not know perfectly well that animals have personalities and minds and feelings."

-Jane Goodall

I have had the great privilege of sharing my life with many incredible animal friends and fur children, so to Muffin, Ace, Slinky, Solomon, Brogan, Norman, Buddy, Charlie and Lambert, thank you for being such compassionate companions and for reminding me to always give love enthusiastically and to never turn down a long walk in the woods. And to my human family, thank you Colleen, Ripley and Rex for providing endless entertaining source material. Love you all so much!

-J.J. JOHNSON

Norman, Thelma, and Louie are the animal loves of my life and I truly thank J.J. for starting that journey by finding a scruffy little light. One of my biggest hopes for my kid loves (Ripley, Rex, Casey, Imogen, and Royce) is that they each have animal friends who inspire them to care and fight for our planet, the home we share with all living beings, just like Jane Garcia and Dr. Jane Goodall do.

-CHRISTIN SIMMS

OUR FUR FAMILIES

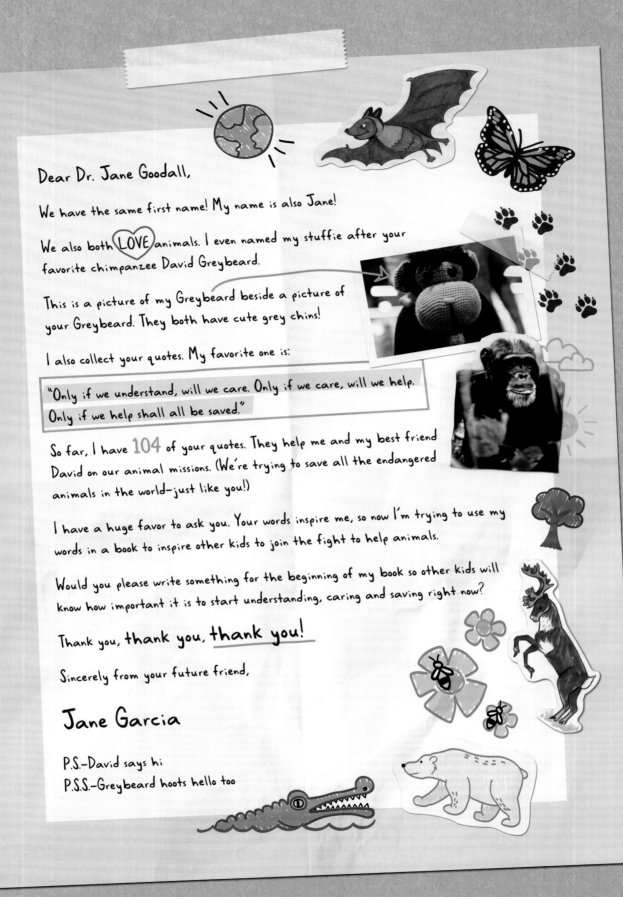

Dear Dr. Jane Goodall,

We have the same first name! My name is also Jane!

We also both LOVE animals. I even named my stuffie after your favorite chimpanzee David Greybeard.

This is a picture of my Greybeard beside a picture of your Greybeard. They both have cute grey chins!

I also collect your quotes. My favorite one is:

"Only if we understand, will we care. Only if we care, will we help. Only if we help shall all be saved."

So far, I have 104 of your quotes. They help me and my best friend David on our animal missions. (We're trying to save all the endangered animals in the world—just like you!)

I have a huge favor to ask you. Your words inspire me, so now I'm trying to use my words in a book to inspire other kids to join the fight to help animals.

Would you please write something for the beginning of my book so other kids will know how important it is to start understanding, caring and saving right now?

Thank you, thank you, **thank you!**

Sincerely from your future friend,

Jane Garcia

P.S.—David says hi
P.S.S.—Greybeard hoots hello too

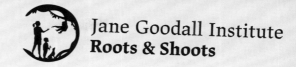

Jane Goodall Institute
Roots & Shoots

Dear Jane Garcia,

Thank you for your letter and pictures. We really do have quite a lot in common, don't we! My David Greybeard was the first chimpanzee in the wild to trust me and he was very special to me and I know he would be proud that you are naming your toy chimp in his honour.

It is great that you are writing a book to inspire the next generation of conservationists. I have met so many young people in my life, children like you Jane, who are really doing wonderful things to make this a better world. They choose projects to help people, animals and the environment.

The message I have for your young readers, is simply this: remember that every day you live you make a difference in the world. So make use of every day to make the world a bit better for animals and people alike. Even if it is only a small difference – hundreds of small differences make for a big difference! You can inspire your friends and family to play their part. It would be great, Jane, if you join my Roots & Shoots program because it involves young people all around the world. Young people like you, who love animals and nature and want to make the world a better place.

Cleaning up a beach

Building bird houses

Learning all about different species

Good luck with all of your future missions.
Your friend,

Jane Goodall

PS – Say hello to your friend Greybeard from me like this "Hoo- hooo- hoooo- hoooooo" (he'll know what it means!)

INTRODUCTION

Hello fellow animal savers!

Did you know that there are over **8,000,000** different types of animals on our planet?

8,000,000!!!!

WOW

There's so many incredible animals to discover! Like these 3 cool, weird animals:

PLATYPUS

AXOLOTI

AYE-AYE

Some of my FAVORITE animals are in this animal guide. Unfortunately, all of them are ENDANGERED which means if we don't do anything they might go EXTINCT, which means they'll be gone forever, which means I'd be really sad.

Did you know that around 150 species of animals go extinct EVERY DAY? Every. Single. Day. 🙁

Some of them we've probably never even heard of before, like these animals:

SPIX'S MACAW

PINTA GIANT TORTOISE

WHY DOES IT MATTER?

Because **ALL** animals are interconnected.

Which includes us PEOPLE.

We're like a GIANT SPIDER WEB. If one part of the web disappears, the whole thing FALLS APART.

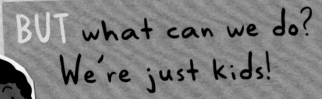

BUT what can we do? We're just kids!

WE CAN DO

SOOOOOOOOOOO MUCH!!!

Just read this quote from my environmental  Dr. Jane Goodall:

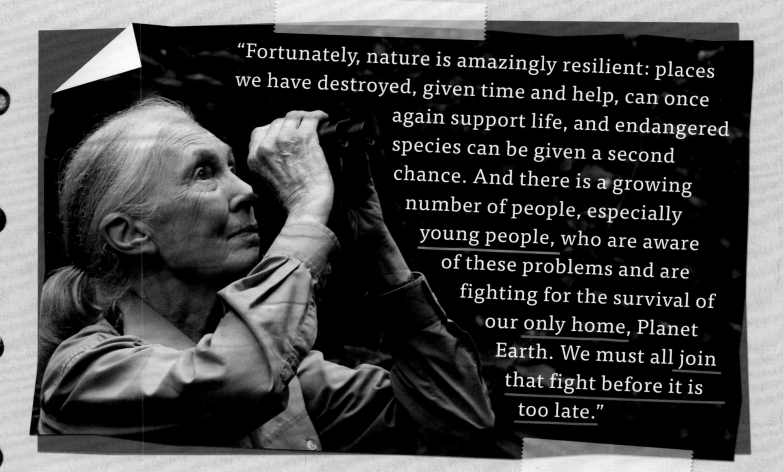

"Fortunately, nature is amazingly resilient: places we have destroyed, given time and help, can once again support life, and endangered species can be given a second chance. And there is a growing number of people, especially young people, who are aware of these problems and are fighting for the survival of our only home, Planet Earth. We must all join that fight before it is too late."

I've UNDERLINED the important parts:

Young people ← That's us.

Only home ← This planet we all share.

Join that fight before it is too late ← Which means there's still time.

← HONEY BEE

<u>BUT</u> we have to work together and quickly.

Throughout this endangered animal guide you'll find:

 Animal <u>MISSIONS</u> with me and my friends David and Greybeard.

And how we solved them.

 <u>INFORMATION</u> about each animal.

Like what their scientific name is, where they live and what they eat.

Because 10 wouldn't be enough!

 ⑪ interesting <u>FACTS</u> and ways you can join the fight to help them.

BUT DON'T STOP THERE!

Use the ideas in this guide AND YOUR OWN BRAND NEW IDEAS to help animals all around you.

Dr. Jane Goodall says:

"The small choices we make each day can lead to the kind of world that we all want for the future."

So start making SMALL choices, then MEDIUM choices, then make BIG choices, then eventually make HUUUUGE choices, choices that are going to inspire people and help animals all over our planet.

Me and the animals are counting on you, so start making good choices!

THANK YOU from ME JANE

TIGER

...AND THANK YOU FROM

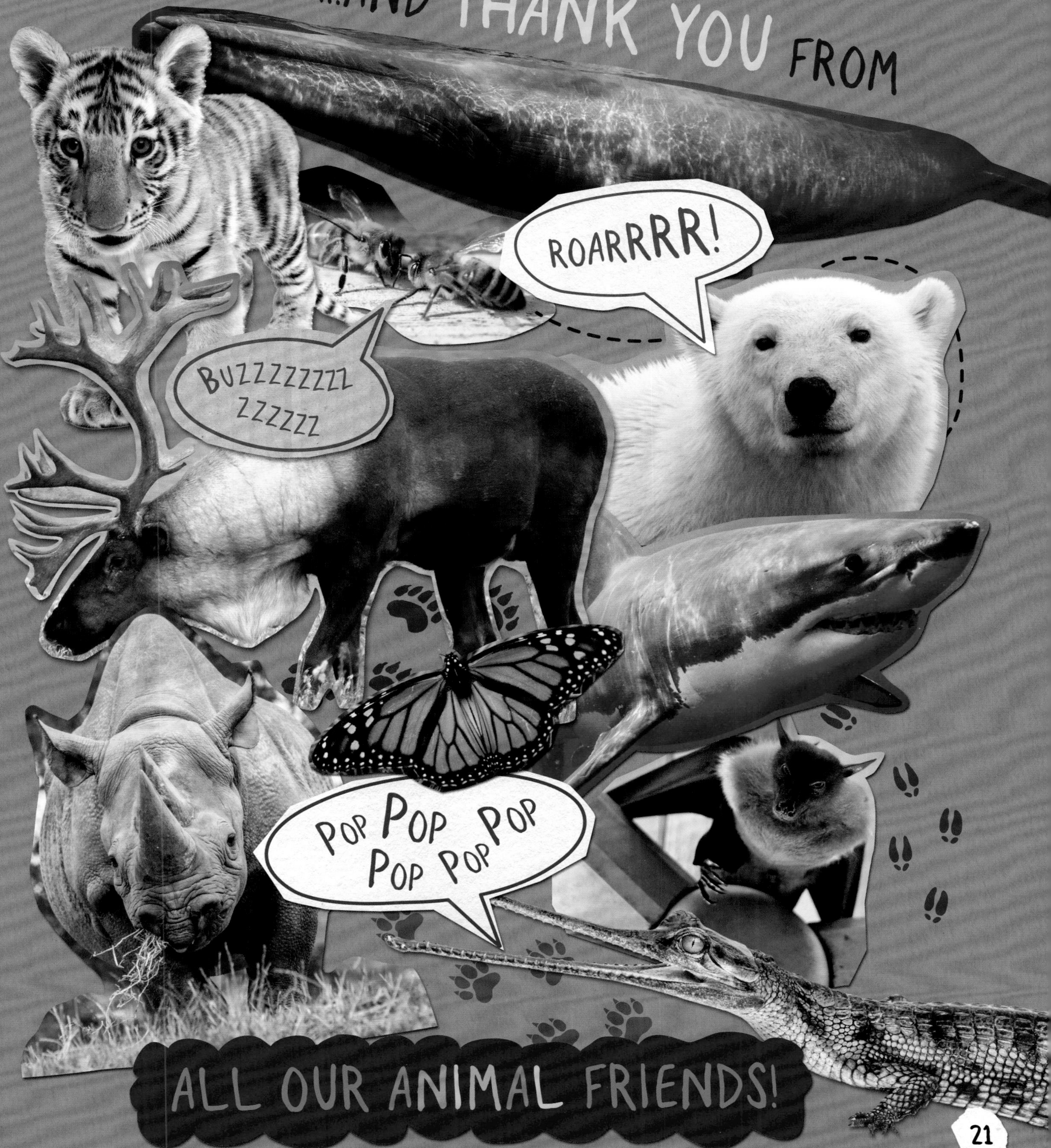

ALL OUR ANIMAL FRIENDS!

North America

South America

Europe

Asia

Africa

Australia

Antarctica

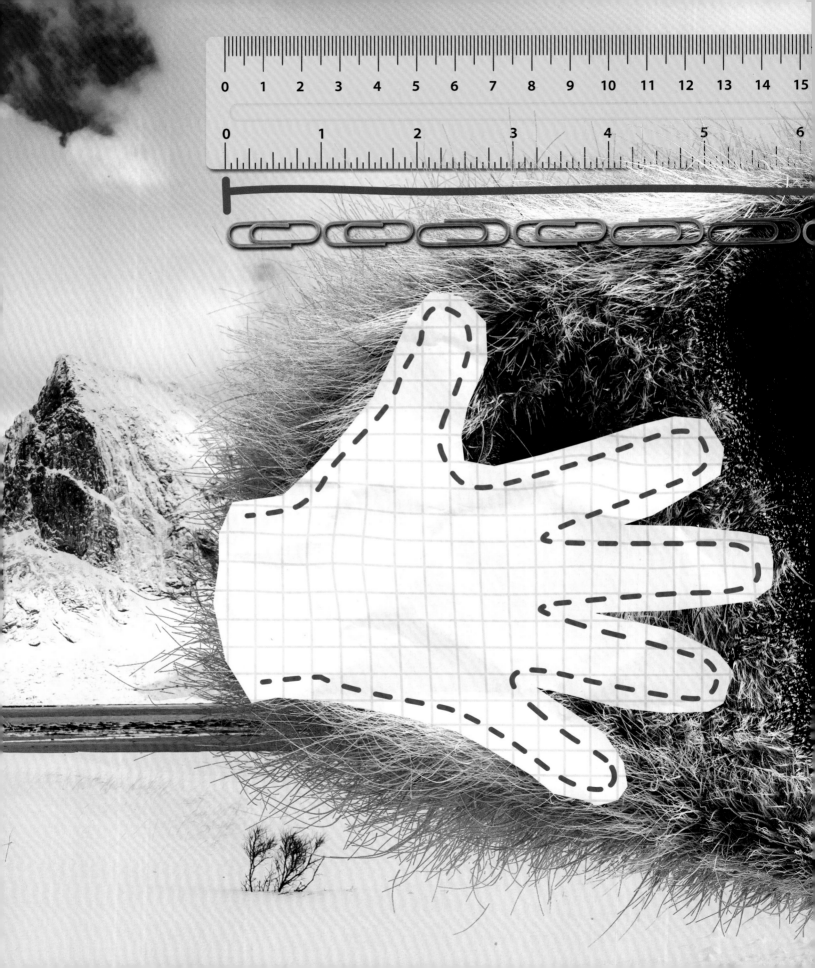

POLAR BEAR

SCIENTIFIC NAME: URSUS MARITIMUS

STATUS

VULNERABLE

WHAT THEY EAT

I'M A CARNIVORE!

WHERE THEY LIVE

Can be found as far south as Newfoundland.

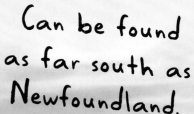

The Arctic Circle

WE NEED TO CHANGE

Open here to find out how BIG a polar bear's PAW is!

MISSION

FIND OUT WHY POLAR BEARS SPEND SO MUCH TIME ALONE.

POLAR BEARS CAN SWIM FOR SEVERAL HOURS BEFORE THEY GET TIRED.

ATTEMPT #1

We're in the Arctic to put a TRACKING COLLAR on a polar bear.

Scientists use tracking collars to see where animals go.

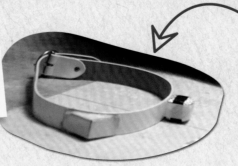

We're going to use one to solve our mission!

But we got interrupted when mom said I needed to finish my breakfast.

My mom reminded me of a Jane Goodall quote I say every morning.

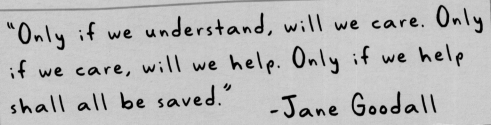

"Only if we understand, will we care. Only if we care, will we help. Only if we help shall all be saved."

-Jane Goodall

We went outside to keep tracking the polar bear.

If polar bears don't have enough food, they eat

GARBAGE ☹

Before we could get the collar on, she ran away, and then I saw my neighbor Mr. Jin. Guess what?

HE DOESN'T RECYCLE!!

REDUCE · REUSE · RECYCLE

SAVE the Earth

ATTEMPT #3

Me and Greybeard found the polar bear sleeping in the hallway!

But instead of putting on the tracking collar...

I <u>PET</u> THE POLAR BEAR!

I probably shouldn't have done that.

AHHHHHHH!

We came up with a plan and tried using the way polar bears hunt to get the tracking collar on the polar bear.

Our Plan

They wait for hours perfectly still, waiting for a seal to pop up.

It's called STILL HUNTING.

I'LL JUST WAIT HERE

AND IT WORKED!

We got the tracking collar on the polar bear!

We discovered that polar bears spend time alone because they don't want to fight for food, and also to take care of their babies.

MISSION: COMPLETE ✓

And I even convinced Mr. Jin to recycle to help the polar bears.

TOP 11 FACTS
— POLAR BEAR —

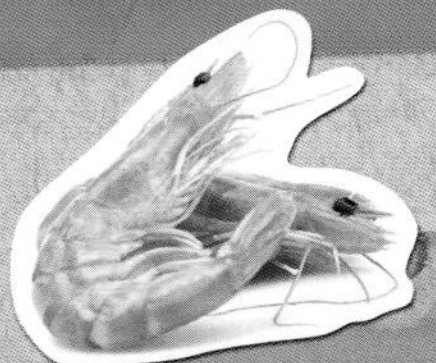

1

Polar bears can go for as long as 8 MONTHS without eating when they hibernate. They survive off all the fat they've built up.

ZZZZZ

2

Polar bears are the largest LAND CARNIVORE!

OUR EARTH MATTERS

③ Polar bears are great SMELLERS. They can smell their food from a long way away.

A group of polar bears is called a pack or a sleuth.

④

⑤ POLAR BEARS CAN LIVE UP TO 30 YEARS

Polar bears aren't white. Their skin is actually black! Their fur is see-through, and it reflects the light, making them look white.

6

7

Polar bears love to swim using their big paws as PADDLES.

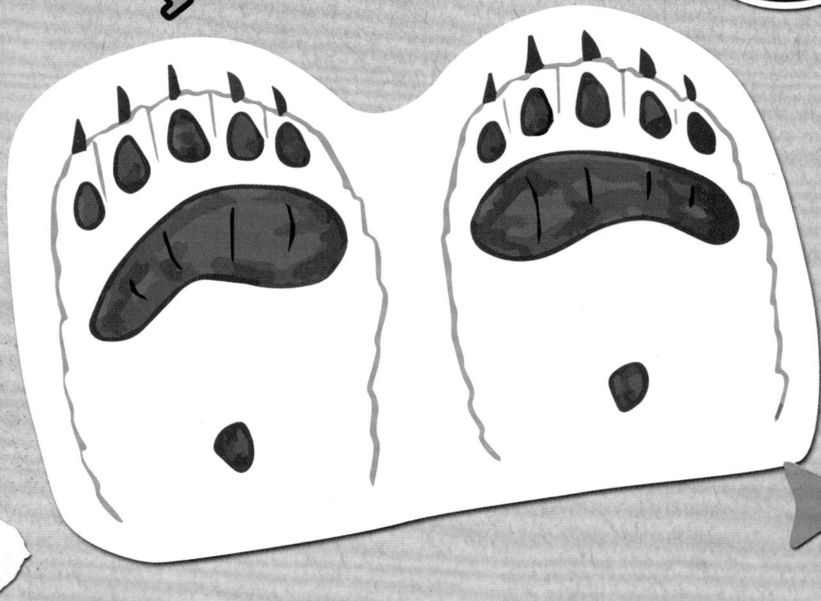

SWIMMING
SWIMMING

Polar bears have little BUMPS on their feet to stop them from slipping on the ice.

8

WILL YOU PLAY WITH ME?

Polar bears wag their heads side to side to tell other polar bears they want to PLAY.

⑨

Polar bears clean themselves by ROLLING in the snow.

⑪

⑩

Polar bear moms usually have TWINS.

How we can Help
POLAR BEARS

Only 30,000 left!

NAME:
Jill Heinerth

OCCUPATION:
Polar bear expert

COOL FACT:
She swum with polar bears!

She also loves Jane Goodall just like I do!
♡♡

Start by reaching out to people who are already helping. There are a lot of them!

I emailed
JILL HEINERTH

Jill told us that one of the biggest problems polar bears have is GLOBAL WARMING. Our planet is getting warmer which means the ice up north is melting.

And guess who needs ice? - POLAR BEARS!!

Polar bears raise their babies and hunt for food on giant ice flows.

They're not the only arctic animal that needs ice, there's also:

Walruses

Sea lions

King eiders

Time to HELP

USE LESS GAS 1

2 I.C.E BANK

BUY LESS

I.C.E BANK
1234 5678 9012 3456
PAULA BEAR

RECYCLE 3

Use less gasoline—so walk or skip or bike or rollerblade or skateboard instead of taking a car.

The exhaust from using gas heats up our planet.

Don't buy so many things and think about everything that you do buy.

Less things means people use less energy and gas to make them.

ASK YOURSELF DO I REALLY NEED THIS????

And if you don't reeeeally need it then don't get it.

Buy LESS and SHARE what you have!

"I'm inspired by young explorers who are out there wanting to make this a better world for all of us."

-Jill Heinerth

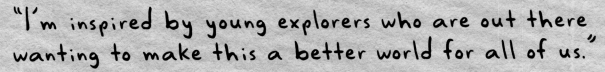

Be like Jill Heinerth and help save the POLAR BEARS!

HOW TO RECYCLE

FIRST STEP: Check in with your local recycling centers.

Double check what they are able to accept!

ALL SORTS OF THINGS CAN BE RECYCLED!

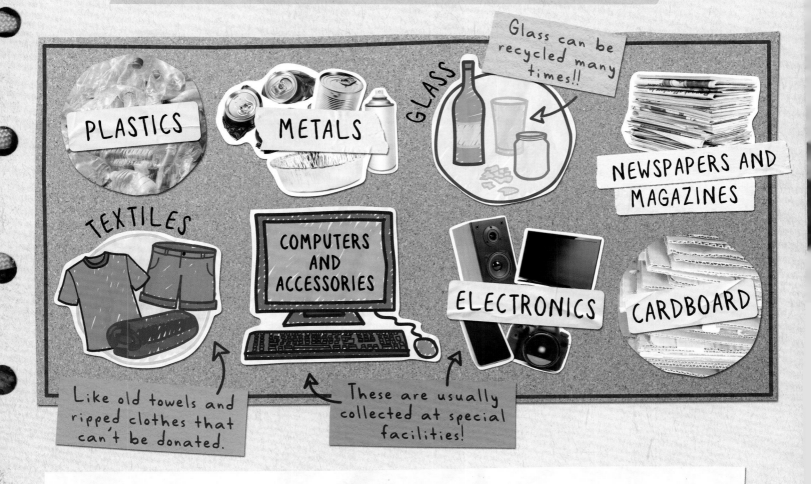

PLASTICS

METALS

GLASS

Glass can be recycled many times!!

NEWSPAPERS AND MAGAZINES

TEXTILES

COMPUTERS AND ACCESSORIES

ELECTRONICS

CARDBOARD

Like old towels and ripped clothes that can't be donated.

These are usually collected at special facilities!

- SORT your paper, plastic, metal, and glass into separate containers.
- RINSE out your bottles and cans before recycling.
- REMOVE caps and lids from all of your containers.

SAY AHHHHHHH!

Hold up the picture of the great white shark behind your head and then take your <u>funniest</u> selfie.

(or most scary!)

Ask a grown-up to help you.

GREAT WHITE SHARK

SCIENTIFIC NAME: CARCHARODON CARCHARIAS

WHERE THEY LIVE

MAP KEY

~~~~~~

Warmer coastal waters

↑
Liked by great white sharks!

PLASTIC BAGS

Open here for a seal's eye view of this shark!

SAVE THE OCEAN FROM PLASTIC POLLUTION

STATUS

VULNERABLE

WHAT THEY EAT

THEY ARE CARNIVORES!

MISSION

FIND OUT WHERE GREAT WHITES SPEND MOST OF THEIR TIME.

GREAT WHITE SHARKS ARE THE WORLD'S LARGEST PREDATORY FISH.

Sharks like to attack their prey from underneath.

ATTEMPT #1

Use a shark cage and a seal decoy to tag a great white with a shark tracker, so we can follow her and see where she spends most of her time.

Seal decoy

Sharks eat:
- Fish
- Seals

Once Greybeard got the seal decoy in the water, a great white shark slammed into the side of the cage!

BANG

And my tata slammed our shopping cart into a display!

Luckily, David was at the grocery store with his dad too.

ATTEMPT #2

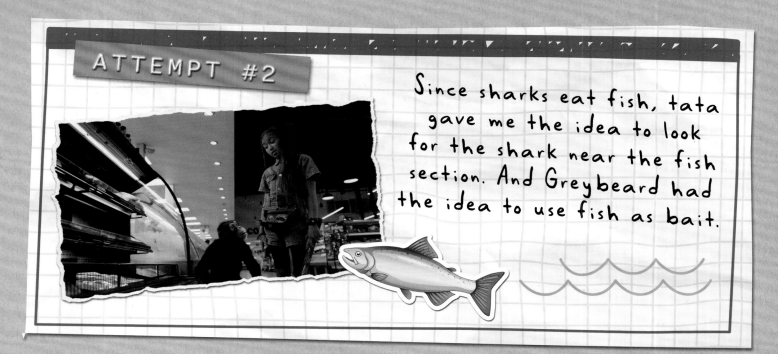

Since sharks eat fish, tata gave me the idea to look for the shark near the fish section. And Greybeard had the idea to use fish as bait.

YUMMY SALMON!

The great white must like salmon because she came after the bait. But she DIDN'T like it when I tried to tag her!

Great whites have one of the strongest bites of any animal in the world.

44

The great white shark chased me all through the grocery store.

Luckily, David saved me with a grocery cart.

David's dad and tata were not happy we made a mess. But I told them that we have to save the sharks.

it's cool to be KIND

SAVE THE PLANET

"The greatest danger to our future is apathy."
-Jane Goodall

So tata helped me figure out that to save the sharks, I should think like one.

ATTEMPT #3

David dressed up as a seal to lure in the shark, so that I could tag it from underneath.

Just like sharks attack their prey!

AND IT WORKED!

While the shark was distracted by seal-David, I tagged it with the tracker!

Which is how we followed the great white shark all the way to the place where they spend most of their time.

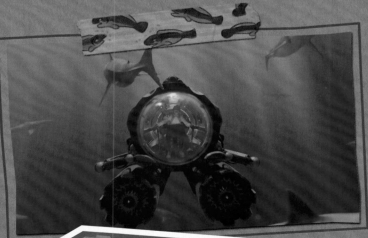

MISSION: COMPLETE ✓

We discovered that's where girl and boy sharks meet up to have their BABIES.

TOP 11 FACTS
— GREAT WHITE SHARK —

SAVE OUR SEAS

1. SHARKS HAVE BEEN AROUND FOR OVER 400 MILLION YEARS!

400 MILLION

2. Sharks RARELY attack people and, if they do, it's by mistake.

OOPS, SORRY I THOUGHT YOU WERE A SEAL!

Great white sharks can jump completely out of the water.

③

NO PLASTIC

④

Great whites have up to <u>300</u> teeth!

SAVE OUR PLANET

⑤

Their teeth are in the shape of TRIANGLES.

6 Great whites can SMELL BLOOD from over 40 football fields away.

x 40

7 They like to surprise their prey from BELOW.

¡SURPRISE!

8 BABY SHARKS ARE CALLED PUPS.

NO PLASTIC

9 Shark pups can **HUNT** as soon as they're born.

10 They're found in EVERY OCEAN in the world except the Antarctic Ocean.

11 Great white sharks can weigh as much as a CAR.

HOW WE CAN HELP
GREAT WHITE SHARKS

One thing you can do is read about or talk to people who are already helping sharks. I had a video chat with **CARLY JACKSON.**

NAME:
Carly Jackson

OCCUPATION:
Marine Biologist

That means—you guessed it—she works with sharks!

She puts little SHARK TAGS on their fins so she can learn more about where sharks go in the ocean.

They measure sharks as they tag them, to see how they're growing!

Carly started liking sharks when she was 5 YEARS OLD after reading a shark book.

Carly told me sharks are way more scared of us than we are of them because we fish too many of them. And they only bite people on ACCIDENT.

Sharks don't eat people-they just sometimes think we look like food!

Carly started a group with her friends called MINORITIES IN SHARK SCIENCES because they didn't see people that looked like them studying sharks. They wanted to change that so they work together to get more diverse people involved.

EVERYONE CAN STUDY AND HELP SHARKS

Carly also told me about a program called **SHARKS FOR KIDS** that helps kids learn about shark conservation.

And about a kid named DYSON CHI who's working to get plastic out of the ocean.

BYE BYE PLASTIC

So many people are trying to help SHARKS, YOU CAN TOO!

One of the things we can do to help sharks is eat less fish and only eat (sustainable) seafood.

Sustainable means it's coming from a place that's environmentally friendly.

CERTIFIED SUSTAINABLE SEAFOOD MSC www.msc.org

MORE FISH in the oceans means more things for sharks to eat which means MORE SHARKS!

"Sharks are fin-tastic!"
-Carly Jackson

This is David's favorite quote!

The Queen

When it's time for a new queen, nurse bees will feed a baby bee (larvae) some royal jelly which they make from the top of their heads. The royal jelly turns the bee into a new queen bee!

HONEY BEE

SCIENTIFIC NAME: APIS MELLIFERA

WHAT THEY EAT

Bees have 2 stomachs!

SAVE THE BEES

TAKE A LOOK INSIDE A BEEHIVE!

STATUS

ENDANGERED

0 1 2 3 4 5 6 7 8 9

0 1 2 3

ACTUAL SIZE

WHERE THEY LIVE

Bees live on every continent except ANTARCTICA.

IDE A BEE HIVE...

HOW MANY BEES DO YOU SEE?

MISSION

FIND OUT WHY WORKER BEES ARE SUDDENLY GOING MISSING.

THE WORKERS ARE DISAPPEARING, AND SCIENTISTS AREN'T SURE WHY!

Bees live in huge COLONIES with one queen, thousands of workers, and a few drones.

ATTEMPT #1

Shrink down, enter a honey bee colony, and figure out why those bees are missing.

One way bees communicate is through smell. That's why our ship is bee-sized and bee-smelled too!

WOAHHHHH!

But before we got into the colony, we got interrupted by a dragonfly chasing us!

And by Curtis throwing rocks at a beehive in the schoolyard.

I HAD TO STOP HIM.

I should have talked to him instead of shoving him.

Next, we used bee smell to call in some bee backup to distract the dragonfly so we could get into the colony.

BEES TO THE RESCUE!

BEES DON'T STING UNLESS THEY'RE PROTECTING THEMSELVES OR THEIR HOMES.

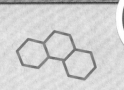

Once we got into the colony, we saw the worker bees really were missing.

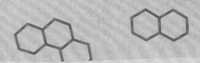

Curtis, can you help us?

And we knew we needed a different kind of backup...

If there's no more BEES, there's no more US. HUMANS NEED BEES.

> "The least I can do is speak out for those who cannot speak for themselves."
> -Jane Goodall

ATTEMPT #3

Then the dragonfly got in the colony and went after the queen bee! We used smell again to make the dragonfly come after us instead!

The average dragonfly is over **6 TIMES BIGGER** then a bee.

QUEEN BEE SMELL ↓

⚠

AND IT WORKED!

We got the dragonfly out of the colony and discovered that worker bees are disappearing because there aren't as many flowers anymore. So, we convinced Curtis to help us dig a bee garden at school to help bees.

MISSION: COMPLETE ✓

TOP 11 FACTS
— HONEY BEE —

People have been BEEKEEPING for over 4500 years!

①

②

Bees make HONEY so they have food over the winter.

③ A BABY BEE looks like this! ⟶

BABY ON BOARD

They are called LARVAE. ↖

④ Bees do a WAGGLE DANCE to let other bees know where the flowers with the most pollen are.

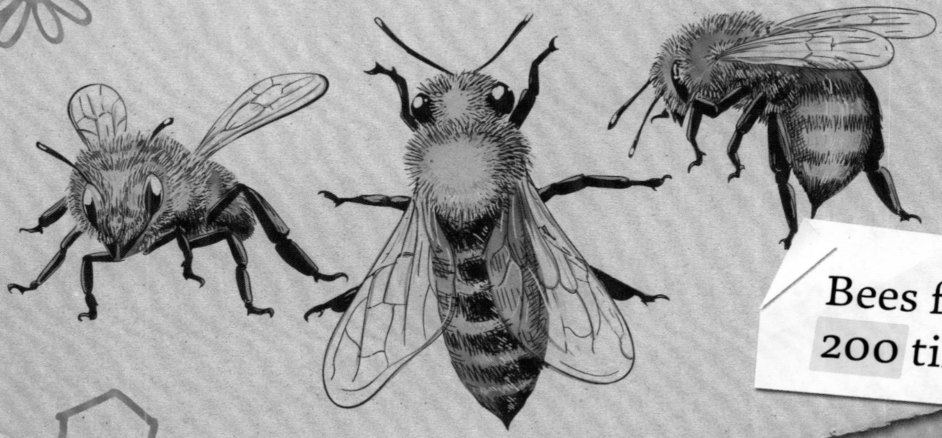

⑤ Bees flap their wings over 200 times a second. !!!

The queen bee can lay up to 2500 eggs a day!

6

Only GIRL bees can sting, BOY bees don't have stingers.

7

There are THREE types of bees in a hive:

8

THE QUEEN
(Top girl boss)

THE DRONES
(All boy bees that help the queen make baby bees)

THE WORKERS
(All girl bees who look for food)

9

Bees live in HIVES that they build themselves.

HOME SWEET HOME

10

BEES HAVE 5 EYES AND 6 LEGS.

11

A beehive can have over 50,000 bees living in it!

HONEY BEES

NAME:
Melanie Kirby

OCCUPATION:
Bee Expert

COOL FACT:
She has her own beehive!

Learn from people who are already helping bees.

I learned from
MELANIE KIRBY

She knows so much about bees that she can wear them like a BEARD.

Only experts should do this—but you could be an expert one day and wear your own bee beard!

Melanie told us that one of the things that's hurting the bees is POOR NUTRITION.

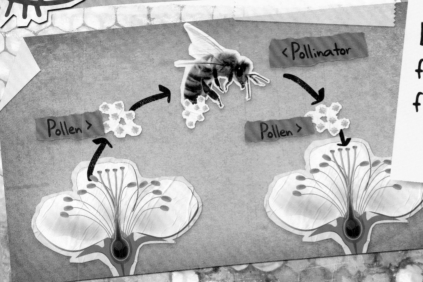

Pollen >

< Pollinator

Pollen >

Bees don't have enough flowers to get POLLEN from so they can't eat and they starve.

BUT WE CAN HELP!

We can plant FLOWERS that they like to get pollen from.

HOW TO PLANT A BEE GARDEN

STEP 1

Get seeds for flowers that grow in your area, then make a seed ball.

CLAY SOIL

STEP 2

Mix soil, the seeds and wet clay or just some water.

STEP 3

The best step-roll it all together until you have a ball.

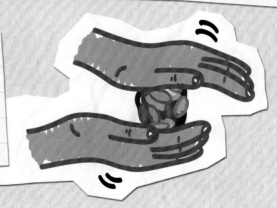

STEP 4

Throw your seed ball wherever there's soil. In a few weeks there will be tasty flowers and the bees will be super happy.

Melanie's not the only person helping bees, there's also:

MARION PIERSON

She started <u>MoHives</u> which works with kids in big cities to plant gardens and make beehives.

DANIELLE and IZZY KLEIN

teach people about how important bees are.

AND SO CAN YOU!

"Like the bees, we can work together to help them!"
-Melanie Kirby

Let's start working together to save BEES today!

GIANT GOLDEN-CROWNED FLYING FOX

SCIENTIFIC NAME: ACERODON JUBATUS

STATUS

ENDANGERED

WHERE THEY LIVE

The Philippines

How BIG is a flying fox's WING?

OPEN HERE TO FIND OUT!

WHAT THEY EAT

I'M A HERBIVORE!

MISSION

Some bats eat INSECTS, FRUIT, MICE, LIZARDS, even other BATS!

But what do flying foxes EAT?

ATTEMPT #1

Skydive into the golden-crowned flying fox's habitat and attach a camera to one of the bats to see what it eats and figure out how to help them.

74

Greybeard and I jumped out of the plane and, while I landed on the ground...

Greybeard landed in a tree next to a bunch of sleeping flying foxes.

Greybeard screamed, which bothered the bats, and then I screamed, which bothered my mom.

But I had to scream again when the wind blew Greybeard and his parachute away!

David and I found him in our neighbor Robin's backyard.

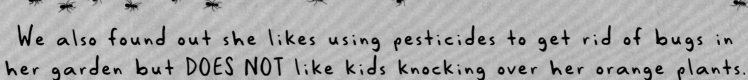

We also found out she likes using pesticides to get rid of bugs in her garden but DOES NOT like kids knocking over her orange plants.

ATTEMPT #2

While we were trying to figure out how to get Greybeard back, the flying fox started chasing us! David thought it was trying to eat him but I wasn't convinced.

When my mom found ants crawling all over us because of the smushed oranges, I thought the flying fox had been trying to eat the ants (i.e. meat) and not us.

But we needed some help to find out for sure...

ONE BAT CAN EAT 1000 BUGS A NIGHT.

"How can we believe it is a good idea to grow our food with poisons?"
-Jane Goodall

We got Robin to put a bat house in her garden, so that bats could stop the bugs and she could stop using pesticides.

AND IT WORKED!

Robin gave me back Greybeard and some oranges for our next mission attempt.

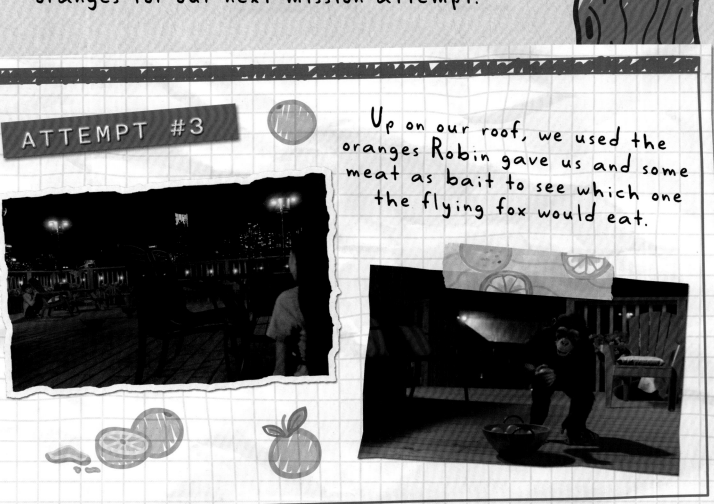

ATTEMPT #3

Up on our roof, we used the oranges Robin gave us and some meat as bait to see which one the flying fox would eat.

Greybeard got hungry for an orange just as the flying fox swooped down!

YUMMM!

For a second, it looked like the flying fox was going after Greybeard, but it just wanted the orange.

We figured out the giant golden-crowned flying fox eats FRUIT, so we went back to the Philippines to plant some more fruit trees!

AND FLY WITH THE FLYING FOXES!

MISSION: COMPLETE ✓

TOP 11 FACTS

— FLYING FOX —

1 Flying foxes live in large groups called colonies or camps.

2 Giant golden-crowned flying foxes got their name from a golden triangle on their heads that looks like a CROWN.

③ Flying foxes like to nap hanging UPSIDE DOWN in trees.

ZZZZZ

④ Giant golden-crowned flying foxes are FRUGIVOROUS.

ONLY EAT FRUIT

⑤ They talk to each other with their CHIRPS.

CHIRP CHIRP CHIRP CHIRP CHIRP CHIRP CHIRP

6 Giant golden-crowned flying foxes only live in the PHILIPPINES.

PHILIPPINES
CONTINENT
ASIA
LANGUAGE
FILIPINO
AREA
300,000 KM²
POPULATION
109.6 MILLIONS

MANILA

7 A baby flying fox is called a PUP.

8 Their predators are PYTHONS, EAGLES, and HUMANS.

9
Flying foxes use their BIG wings to keep cool on hot days.

They fan themselves with their wings.

10
The giant golden-crowned flying fox is the biggest of all bats.

COMMON VAMPIRE BAT

HOARY BAT

11
Even though they're the biggest and have massive wings, they only weigh as much as a pineapple!

HOW WE CAN HELP

FLYING FOXES

Get ideas from other people who are already helping flying foxes.

I talked with **LISA PAGUNTALAN.**

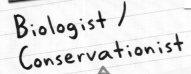

NAME:
Lisa Paguntalan

OCCUPATION:

Biologist /
Conservationist

She works in the Philippines trying to save these cute, endangered bats! ♡ ♡

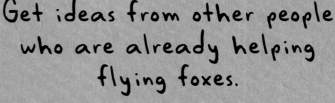

The Philippines is here!

She told us the fruit flying foxes love the most is FIGS. 79 percent of what they eat is figs! And the figs love the flying foxes too because the bats help spread their seeds in their poo. ← Called GUANO.

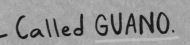

She also told us there are only 10,000 to 20,000 flying foxes left in the wild because we're <u>destroying</u> where they live.

<u>BUT</u> people are starting to work together to help protect the bats.

Lisa helps teach people how to count the bats using a SPOTTING SCOPE.

If we know how many bats are left, we can see if what we're doing to help them is working or not.

Flying foxes live together in ROOSTING COLONIES.

A bat roost means any place that wild bats use for SHELTER or PROTECTION.

One of the big things we can do to help is to
TALK ABOUT BATS!

Share <u>good stories</u> about bats with your friends, your teachers, your parents, EVERYONE!

Like how they plant figs!

Or how cute they are!

Try to change the mind of anyone who is afraid of bats.

You can also build a bat house and put it in your backyard or neighborhood to help bats have a safe place to live in your community!

♥HOME♥
SWEET
♥HOME♥

HOW TO BUILD A BAT HOUSE!

Find or make a RECTANGULAR BOX that's about the size of a mailbox.

Add NOTCHES inside for the bats to climb (like a ladder!)

HANG it on a TREE at least the length of one grown-up away from the ground with the opening on the bottom.

"A loss of one Philippines species is not just a loss of biodiversity of the Philippines, it is the loss of the world. Because we are all connected."

-Lisa P.

So HELP BATS wherever you live!

The gharial's skull is as long as 4 PENCILS!

GHARIAL

SCIENTIFIC NAME: GAVIALIS GANGETICUS

WHERE THEY LIVE

Gharials live in the Girwa and Chambal rivers in India and the Rapti-Narayani river in Nepal.

How LONG is a gharial's NOSE?

OPEN THE MIDDLE FLAP TO FIND OUT!

⚠ STATUS ⚠

CRITICALLY 🙁

ENDANGERED

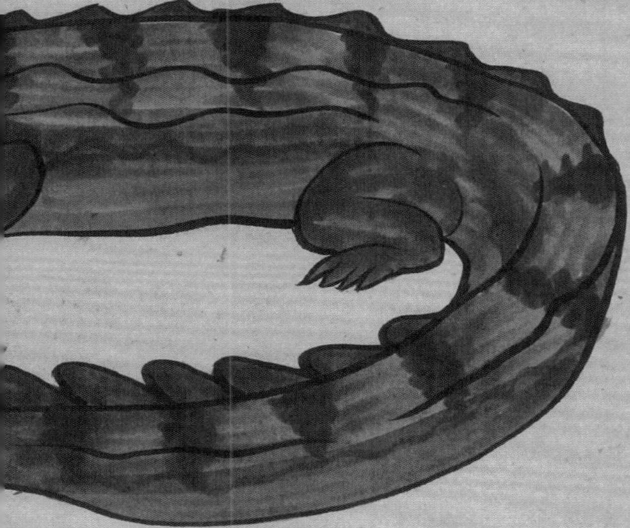

⚠

THEY ARE CARNIVORES!

WHAT THEY EAT

89

MISSION

FIND OUT WHAT THE STRANGE BULB AT THE END OF THE GHARIAL'S NOSE IS USED FOR.

Gharials are crocodiles that have lived since dinosaurs roamed the earth.

But now there are only a little over 600 of them left in the WHOLE WORLD.

RAWR

ATTEMPT #1

Search for a gharial in the river where they live and figure out why they have bulbs at the end of their noses.

We found a gharial on the side of the river, but as soon as it saw us, it jumped into the river and started swimming away!

WE HAD TO FOLLOW THAT **NOSE!**

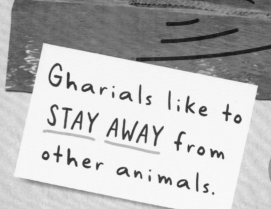

Gharials like to STAY AWAY from other animals.

AHHHHHHHHHH

Before we could get close to the gharial, we got close to a waterfall instead!

My mom wanted us to help her and our neighbor Andre with some chores at our co-op's pool.

WE WERE NOT IMPRESSED.

ATTEMPT #2

SPLASH!!!!

We accidentally splashed my mom.

But we had to get back to searching for the gharial.

We had to go home to get dry. My mom turned on ALL the lights, even though it was daytime. I turned them off but she didn't like that.

Luckily, I knew where to turn for some good advice:

"Every individual matters. Every individual has a role to play. Every individual makes a difference."
—Jane Goodall

ATTEMPT #3

David searched the park.

Next time we tried to follow the gharial, we lost track of it and had to split up.

I searched the pool.

93

AND IT WORKED!

We BOTH found a GHARIAL!

POP POP POP POP POP

POP POP POP

They were using the bulbs on their noses to talk to each other! But guess what? We saw another gharial!

But this one didn't have a bulb on its nose, because it was a girl! The boy gharials were both trying to talk to her too, but she only wanted to talk to one of them.

XOXO ♥ 😘

After my mom and I made up, she and Andre helped us figure out that the boy gharials were trying to impress the girl. Just like Andre was trying to impress my mom.

MISSION: COMPLETE ✓

Good teams TALK to each other, and that's how the girl and boy gharials will make sure there's more gharials on the river soon.

TOP 11 FACTS
— GHARIAL —

① GHARIALS ARE RELATED TO DINOSAURS.

GO GREEN

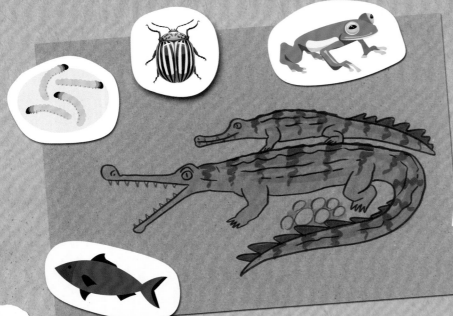

② Young gharials eat INSECTS, LARVAE, and small FROGS.

Grown-ups mostly eat FISH.

③ They have WEBBED FEET to help them swim fast through water.

④ Gharials are very SHY and hide from humans.

GHARIALS ARE FAST IN THE WATER...

⑤

...BUT REALLLLLLLY SLOW ON LAND.

97

6 Gharials live in Nepal and Northern India.

7 GHARIALS LIKE TO LIE IN THE SUN TO GET WARM.

8 Girl gharials can lay as many as 60 EGGS in their nests. When the babies are born, sometimes the boy gharials give them a piggyback ride.

9 Gharials have 110 razor-sharp teeth, which help them catch slippery fish.

10 All gharials have long, skinny snouts, but the boys have a ROUND BULB at the end.

Gavialis gangeticus. Indian Crocodile or Gavial.

Crocodilus vulgaris. Nile Crocodile.

Jacare sclerops. Spectacled Alligator

11 Gharials are one of the LONGEST members of the crocodile family.

99

GHARIALS

Search for other people who are saving gharials.

David and I talked to RU SOMAWEERA.

Which means he studies REPTILES

NAME:

Ru Somaweera

OCCUPATION:

Herpetologist

He told us gharials are GREAT PARENTS and that the dads look after the babies and keep them safe from predators.

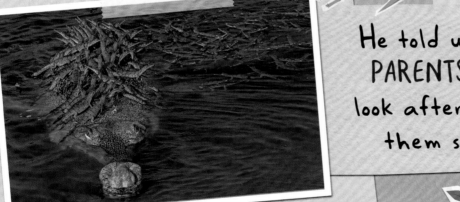

They even let them ride on their backs!

A predator might try to attack this baby.

But not this grown-up!

BEST DAD EVER!

My dad has the largest teeth!

My dad is stronger than your dad!

My dad is the greatest!

My dad has the most teeth!

Ru started loving reptiles when he was a kid. He said he found them MYSTERIOUS, MESMERIZING AND MISUNDERSTOOD.

Like how some people might think they're not good parents BUT THEY ARE.

Gharials are in trouble because they're losing their (HABITAT). ← Where they live

To help them, Ru said we should tell everyone how important they are.

Gharials are (APEX PREDATORS). ← Which means they're at the top of the food chain

BUGS AND PLANTS → FISH → GHARIALS

Without gharials there, the whole chain falls apart.

Gharials are not the only good dads. So is Ru!

Ru's son RAYHAN is one of the youngest Australians to ever write a scientific paper.

Ru also told us we can help gharials by RAISING MONEY.

PART OF YOUR ALLOWANCE

BAKE SALE

Bake SALE

sept.13
3 PM-8 PM

15 Sweet Street

MAKE AND SELL GHARIAL PICTURES

And donate what you make to charities that are helping gharials.

"Gharials are cold blooded but they can be really warm hearted."
-Ru Somaweera

"Remember it's not only the cute and cuddly animals that matter."
-Rayhan Somaweera

GHARIALS matter too, so let's do EVERYTHING we can to help save them!

Did you know whales are COLOR blind? They can only see in different shades of GRAY.

WHALE VISION

HUMAN VISION

BLUE WHALE

SCIENTIFIC NAME: BALAENOPTERA MUSCULUS

WHERE THEY LIVE

Arctic Ocean

Atlantic Ocean

Pacific Ocean

Indian Ocean

Pacific Ocean

Southern Ocean

Blue whales are found in every ocean except the ARCTIC OCEAN.

SAVE THE WHALES

How BIG is a whale's EYE?

OPEN HERE TO FIND OUT!

ENDANGERED

I'M A CARNIVORE!

WHAT THEY EAT

Blue whales eat krill

They have 3 stomachs!

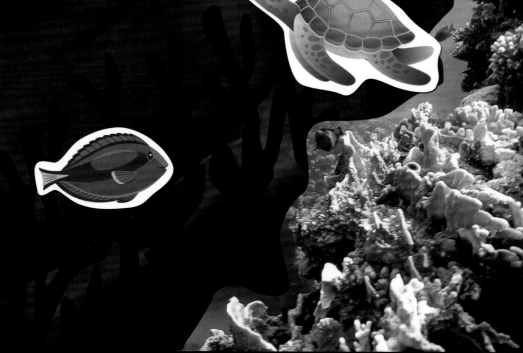

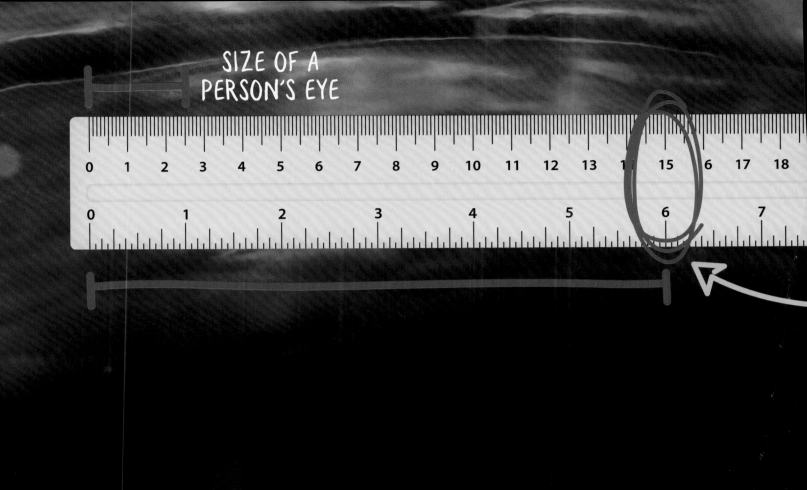

SIZE OF A
PERSON'S EYE

FIND OUT WHY BLUE WHALES SING.

Blue whales are bigger than any other animal that has ever existed.

BIGGER THAN THE BIGGEST DINOSAUR!

But scientists still aren't sure WHY they sing.

106

ATTEMPT #1

Go deep into the ocean in a submarine to find a blue whale and figure out why they sing.

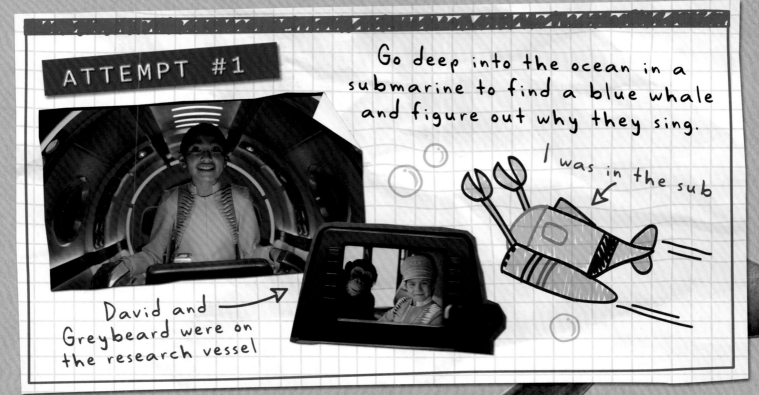

I was in the sub

David and Greybeard were on the research vessel

We heard a whale song and then we saw a whole cloud of krill.

MILLIONS & MILLIONS OF THEM!

And then a blue whale ATE them!

Krill are BIO-LUMINESCENT -they light up.

Before we could figure out why blue whales sing, we saw a fishing net in the whale's mouth!

I HAD TO GET IT OUT.

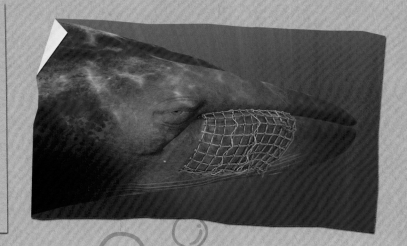

BUT THAT DIDN'T GO SO WELL!

Plus I had to take the laundry upstairs. I met my neighbor Toni in the elevator. She loves to sing (and to litter).

DON'T LITTER!!

I told her why that was bad, which David doesn't think she loved.

ATTEMPT #2

David, Greybeard and I found the blue whale over our roof and tried to get the fishing net out of his mouth.

But we couldn't reach.

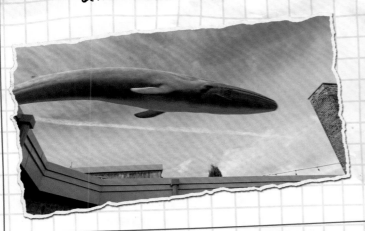

> "Change happens by listening and then starting a dialogue with the people who are doing something you don't believe is right."
> —Jane Goodall

We needed a new plan, and some help.

ATTEMPT #3

Toni sang to the blue whale. She got him to sing back to her so we could get the fishing net out of his mouth! (She also stopped littering.)

AND IT WORKED!

Once the blue whale started singing, another blue whale showed up.

AND MORE KRILL LIT UP!

We discovered that blue whales sing to light up the krill so they can find them and eat them!

MISSION: COMPLETE ✓

TOP 11 FACTS
— BLUE WHALE —

① Blue whales are not only the largest animal on the planet they're also the loudest.

LOUDER THAN A JET ENGINE!

② Girl blue whales are BIGGER than boy blue whales.

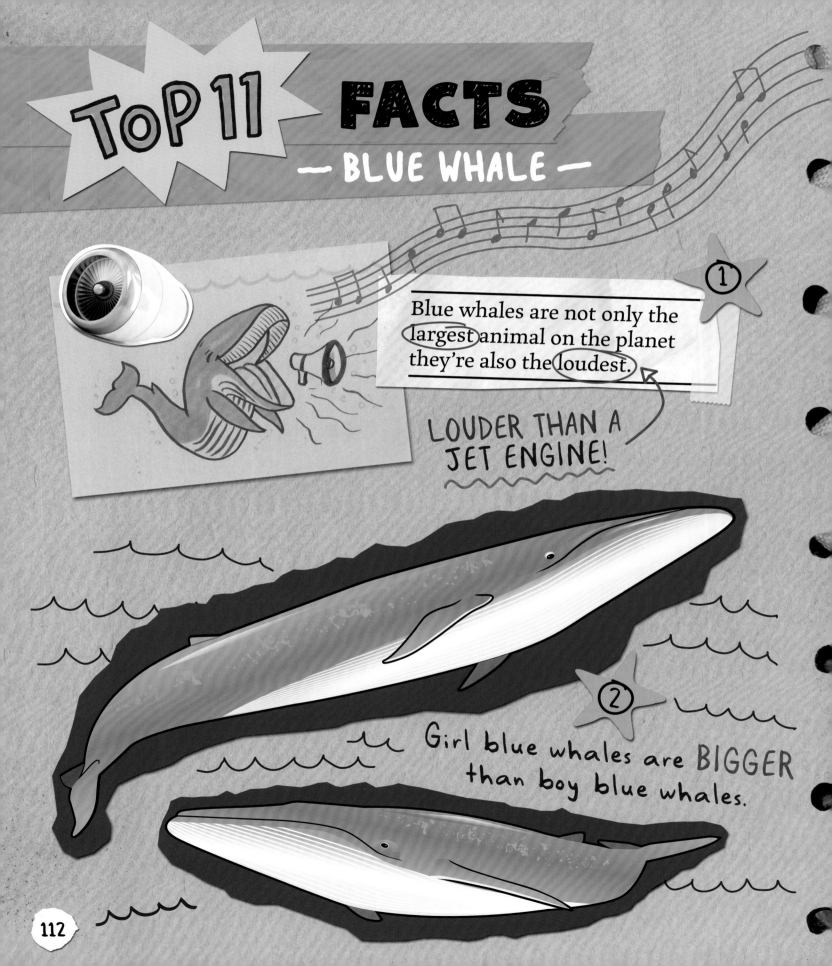

③ A group of blue whales is called a POD.

USE LESS PLASTIC

④ A baby blue whale is called a CALF.

The same as a baby cow.

SAVE THE WHALES

⑤ A blue whale's tongue weighs as much as a TRICERATOPS.

⑥ Blue whales breathe through a BLOWHOLE on the top of their body.

⑦ A blue whale is as long as three T-REXES.

⑧ Blue whales can live up to a 110 years old!

HOW WE CAN HELP

BLUE WHALES

Find other blue whale helpers!

I found DR. ASHA DE VOS.

NAME:

Dr. Asha de Vos

OCCUPATION:

Marine Biologist

She studies blue whales.

FUN FACT:

She started loving Blue Whales when she was only SIX YEARS OLD!

That's the same age as David's sister Millie!

ASHA

MILLIE

She started her own group to help blue whales called OCEANSWELL because there weren't any Marine Biologists in her country when she was younger.

Oceanswell
Oceans for all, forever

Asha wants Oceanswell to INSPIRE kids to learn about and save the oceans.

KIDS LIKE US!

Asha told us that some of the main threats blue whales face are hitting boats, getting tangled in fishing nets and the NOISE from SUBMARINES and SHIP ENGINES.

Sometimes it's so NOISY underwater that they can't find their FOOD or their FRIENDS.

Time to HELP

Tell everyone you know about BLUE WHALES and what's hurting them. The more people know, the more they'll want to HELP them.

DON'T LITTER and use LESS plastic bottles.

Litter left on the ground can sometimes end up in the ocean and HURT underwater animals.

The LESS PLASTIC you use, the less chance it has of ending up in the ocean.

Use a REUSABLE water bottle and ask other people to do the same.

Even REUSING the same plastic water bottle is a start.

"If we truly want to save our oceans, every coastline needs a local hero."

-Dr. Asha de Vos

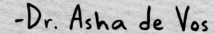

You could be that HERO!

SUPER ZOOM!

Butterfly wings are super STRONG.

Young monarchs wings are vivid ORANGE!

MONARCH BUTTERFLY

SCIENTIFIC NAME: DANAUS PLEXIPPUS

STATUS

⚠ ⚠

ENDANGERED

PLANT MORE

North, Central, and South America.

They can also be found in Australia, the Pacific islands, Indonesia, Spain and Portugal.

OPEN to see a butterfly wing up close!

WHAT THEY EAT

Nectar produced by flowers

Over time they can lose these cells (scratches from thorny plants, high winds, escaping from spider webs!) so they end up losing their color.

SUPER SUPER SUPER ZOOOOOOM!

Monarch wings are covered in these tiny SCALES.

SUPER SUPER ZOOM!

MISSION

TAG A MONARCH BUTTERFLY TO FIND OUT WHERE IT NEEDS HELP ON ITS <u>JOURNEY.</u>

Every year monarch butterflies travel between Mexico, the US, and Canada to have their babies.

BUTTERFLIES FLY DURING THE DAY AND REST AT NIGHT.

ATTEMPT #1

Shrink down, tag a monarch butterfly and follow it.

Butterflies use WIND to help them travel long distances.

Greybeard went out on the edge of our ship to tag a butterfly...

* * AND IT WORKED! * *

But then Greybeard FELL DOWN ...all the WAY DOWN

...to MR. PATEL'S BALCONY!

123

Mr. Patel told me caterpillars, which are baby monarch butterflies, need to eat a plant called milkweed. But he didn't want to plant any because he doesn't like them!

Milkweed

ATTEMPT #2

If Mr. Patel wasn't going to help the monarchs, we had to! We rode the wind to get to the butterfly Greybeard had tagged. But when we found her, she was dead.

Even though it made me sad that the butterfly didn't make it, my mom reminded me of some really good advice...

> "If people don't agree with you, the important thing is to listen to them. But if you've listened to them carefully and you still think that you're right, then have the courage of your convictions."
>
> —Jane Goodall

I knew I had to convince Mr. Patel to plant some milkweed!

I told Mr. Patel we have to LISTEN to each other if we're going to save animals and plants, and he told me even though monarchs don't all make their long migration, they take the journey so that their kids will.

WHICH GAVE ME AN IDEA!

We went looking for caterpillars. We didn't find any, but we did find a CHRYSALIS!

Caterpillars make a chrysalis around themselves so they can transform into a butterfly...

Which we TAGGED!

And Mr. Patel planted some milkweed!

This new butterfly didn't make it either, but her EGGS did!

And we discovered that butterflies start the journey but it is their kids' kids who finish it. We can help them by planting MILKWEED along the way.

MISSION: COMPLETE

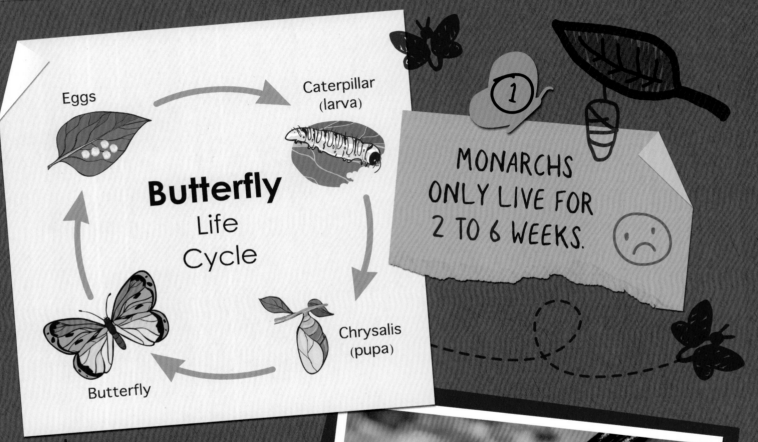

Butterfly Life Cycle

Eggs

Caterpillar (larva)

Chrysalis (pupa)

Butterfly

① MONARCHS ONLY LIVE FOR 2 TO 6 WEEKS.

② Monarchs can't bite, instead they use their TONGUE like a straw to slurp up their food.

Sluuuuurrp

Monarchs use the SUN to help them know where to go.

3

4

Monarch butterflies flap their wings 5 to 12 times a second.

A girl monarch can lay up to 500 eggs in her life!

5

⑥ Monarchs taste with the hairs on their LEGS and FEET.

YUMMY!

⑦ Monarchs smell with their ANTENNAE.

⑧ MONARCHS ARE POISONOUS.

Not to humans but to predators like frogs, mice and birds.

130

Monarchs fly all the way from Mexico through the US to Canada and back each year!

⑨

⑩ Boy monarchs have DARK SPOTS on their back wings, girls don't.

⑪ Butterflies start out as LARVAE.

Before becoming CATERPILLARS.

Then they become BUTTERFLIES.

MONARCH BUTTERFLIES

NAME:

Dr. Patrick Guerra

OCCUPATION:

(Neuroscientist) and Butterfly Expert

That's someone who studies brains!!

First thing: Contact other people who love butterflies.

I contacted
DR. PATRICK GUERRA

he's a butterfly expert who has dedicated his life to helping them.

He told us butterfly brains are only as big as a **PIN HEAD!** But somehow that small brain knows how to transform from a caterpillar to a butterfly and how to fly from **CANADA** through the **UNITED STATES** to **MEXICO** and back again.

He also told us that monarchs' lives are
<u>GETTING HARDER.</u>

With more cities being built, there's less fields that they're flying over. LESS FIELDS means LESS FLOWERS and MILKWEED which the butterflies need to eat and lay their eggs on.

But there's hope. LOTS OF HOPE!

Patrick told us about tons of people trying to help the monarch butterflies, like:

GENEVIEVE LEROUX, she's 16 and lives in Canada and is already a butterfly conservationist.

That means someone who helps butterflies

She TAGS them so researchers can understand more about how butterflies live.

If we can understand, we can care. If we can care, **WE CAN SAVE THEM!**

There's also **AIDEN WANG.** He's been planting milkweed in the United States.

That's the only thing baby caterpillars EAT.

The MORE HE PLANTS, the MORE THEY CAN EAT, the MORE BUTTERFLIES there will be.

Patrick also told us about JOEL MORANO from Mexico who started his own not for profit to help protect the forest for butterflies.

That means they're not trying to make money, they just want to help something.

People all over CANADA, the UNITED STATES and MEXICO are working together to save monarch butterflies.

You can tag BUTTERFLIES, plant MILKWEED and protect FORESTS too! Just like Genevieve, Aiden and Joel!

"It doesn't matter what you do, whether it's really small or really large, it all adds up."

-Dr. Patrick Guerra

Do something really small or really large today! The butterflies are COUNTING on you!

BLACK RHINO

SCIENTIFIC NAME: DICEROS BICORNIS

!

Less than 6,000 left!

STATUS
CRITICALLY
ENDANGERED

WHAT THEY EAT

I'M A HERBIVORE!

HOW LONG IS A BLACK RHINO'S HORN?

Open here to find out!

WHERE THEY LIVE

Eastern and Southern Africa

MISSION

FIND OUT WHY BLACK RHINOS LET RED-BILLED OXPECKERS SIT ON THEIR BACKS ALL DAY.

BLACK RHINOS ARE ILLEGALLY HUNTED FOR THEIR HORNS.

NO POACHING

Oxpecker

They're not very friendly, except to this little bird. And we need to understand why!

ATTEMPT #1

Sneak up really close to the black rhino and see why the oxpecker is allowed to sit on him.

HI, DAVID HERE! WE DID NEED A BETTER PLAN.

But David kept saying we needed a better plan.

And the rhino heard us and started chasing us!!!

BLACK RHINOS ARE REALLY GOOD AT HEARING.

And I tripped and fell, which hurt (but not that much).

DAVID AGAIN, SEE I TOLD YOU JANE, WE NEEDED A BETTER PLAN.

OUCH!!!

I didn't think so and we decided to work on the rhino mission separately.

THAT MEANS WE HAD A FIGHT.

Luckily, our neighbor Mrs. Joseph had some good ideas.

ATTEMPT #2

Mrs. Joseph told me it helps to have a second pair of eyes and... guess what?!

The oxpecker squawked when he saw me and Greybeard sneaking up and then the rhino chased us! I think it was a warning!

SQUAWK!!

HHHHHHH

Is <u>that</u> why the rhino lets it sit on his back?

BLACK RHINOS EAT:

OM NOM NOM

MUNCH MUNCH

- Leafy greens
- Woody twigs
- Succulents

ATTEMPT #3

ALSO KNOWN AS DAVID'S ATTEMPT

MRS. JOSEPH TOLD ME THAT THERE WERE SOME LEAFY GREENS BY THE GARDEN SHED. I DECIDED TO USE THEM AS RHINO BAIT.

AND IT WORKED!

HEAR THAT, JANE!

I GOT CLOSE ENOUGH TO SEE THE BLACK RHINO WAS COVERED IN BUGS AND THE OXPECKER WAS EATING THEM.

GROSS!

IS THAT WHY THE RHINO LETS IT SIT ON HIS BACK?

We didn't know how to figure it out for sure.

MRS. JOSEPH HELPED US AGAIN!

 She reminded me that Jane Goodall said this...

"Each one of us must take responsibility for our own lives, and above all, show respect and love for living things around us, especially each other."

-Jane Goodall

So, BOTH of us took responsibility for our fight.

THAT MEANS WE MADE UP! AND CAME UP WITH A NEW PLAN!

SQUAWK!!

We got the red-billed oxpecker to warn the black rhino again, and we used leafy greens as bait.

We saw that it does eat the bugs off the rhino's back to keep him clean.

But the main reason the black rhino lets the red-billed oxpecker sit on his back is they make a great team.

MISSION: COMPLETE ✓

Hoot hoot hoot! Just like we do!

TOP 11 FACTS
— BLACK RHINO —

1 Black rhinos can live up to 50 years in the wild.

GO GREEN

2 BLACK RHINOS USE THEIR SENSE OF SMELL TO DETECT PREDATORS.

3 Black rhino horns are kind of like HUMAN FINGERNAILS

...if they break off, they grow back.

4 A group of rhinos is called a CRASH.

CRASH!

PLANT MORE TREES

5 A black rhino can weigh as much as a PICKUP TRUCK.

6 Black rhinos run their FASTEST on the tips of their toes.

7 Baby rhinos stay with their moms until they get a brother or sister...

which is when they're about TWO years old and fully grown.

8 Black rhinos mostly like to be on their own except for mom rhinos who stay with their adorable BABIES.

9

BLACK RHINOS ARE HERBIVORES.

They eat over 200 kinds of leafy plants, branches, bushes, and fruit.

Rhinos use their horns for DEFENSE, looking TOUGH, and DIGGING for food.

10

The longest known black rhino horn is almost as tall as a REFRIGERATOR.

11

BLACK RHINOS AREN'T ACTUALLY BLACK-THEY'RE DARK GRAY.

HOW WE CAN HELP
BLACK RHINOS

Learn as much as you can from people who are already doing everything they can to save BLACK RHINOS.

We learned from DR. MATHEW MUTINDA

NAME:

Dr. Mathew Mutinda

OCCUPATION:

Wildlife veterinarian

He's an expert on black rhinos!

He told us how the black rhino and the RED-BILLED OXPECKER have a symbiotic relationship.

That's when two species benefit from each other.

The rhino gets CLEANED and gets warnings from the oxpecker and the oxpecker gets FOOD from the rhino's back.

Pretty GOOD DEAL!

Mathew helps look after injured or abandoned BABY RHINOS.

Like KATUI.

He even gets to feed them from a huge milk bottle.

When they get older, they get released BACK INTO THE WILD.

Mathew told us there are 3 reasons black rhinos are endangered:

1) POACHING: people killing rhinos for their HORNS.

2) HABITAT LOSS: more farms means less places for the rhino—NO HOME, NO RHINOS.

3) CLIMATE CHANGE: less rainfall, less food, less rhinos.

To help, Mathew told us to join a CONSERVATION CLUB or start our own.

We're going to start a rhino conservation club, you should too! And get your friends to JOIN!

"Future generations of conservators are going to save the world."
-Dr. Mathew Mutinda

That's you and me, so let's get started saving the world!

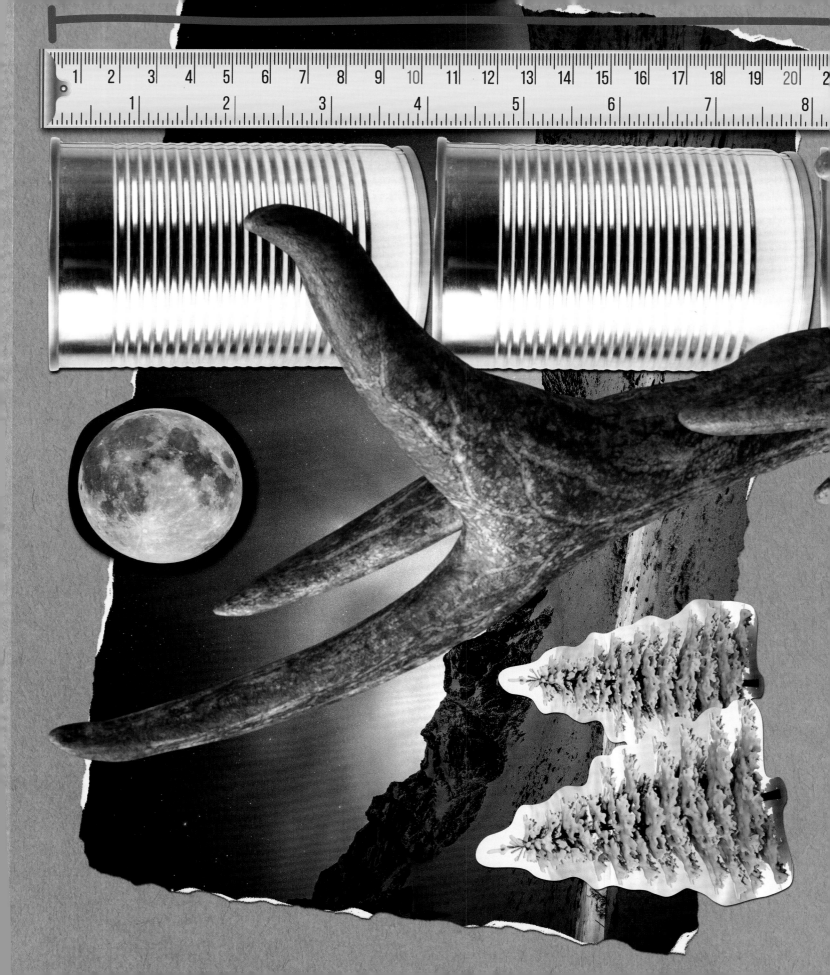

Hold this page up over your head while looking in a MIRROR to see what you look like with an antler! _____

CARIBOU

SCIENTIFIC NAME: RANGIFER TARANDUS

STATUS ⚠

VULNERABLE

WHERE THEY LIVE

MAP KEY

Arctic tundra, mountain tundra, and northern forests of North America, Russia, and Scandinavia.

How BIG are a female caribou's antlers?

OPEN HERE TO FIND OUT!

WHAT THEY EAT

STOP CLIMATE CHANGE

I'M A HERBIVORE!

A caribou antler is as tall as 5 SOUP CANS!

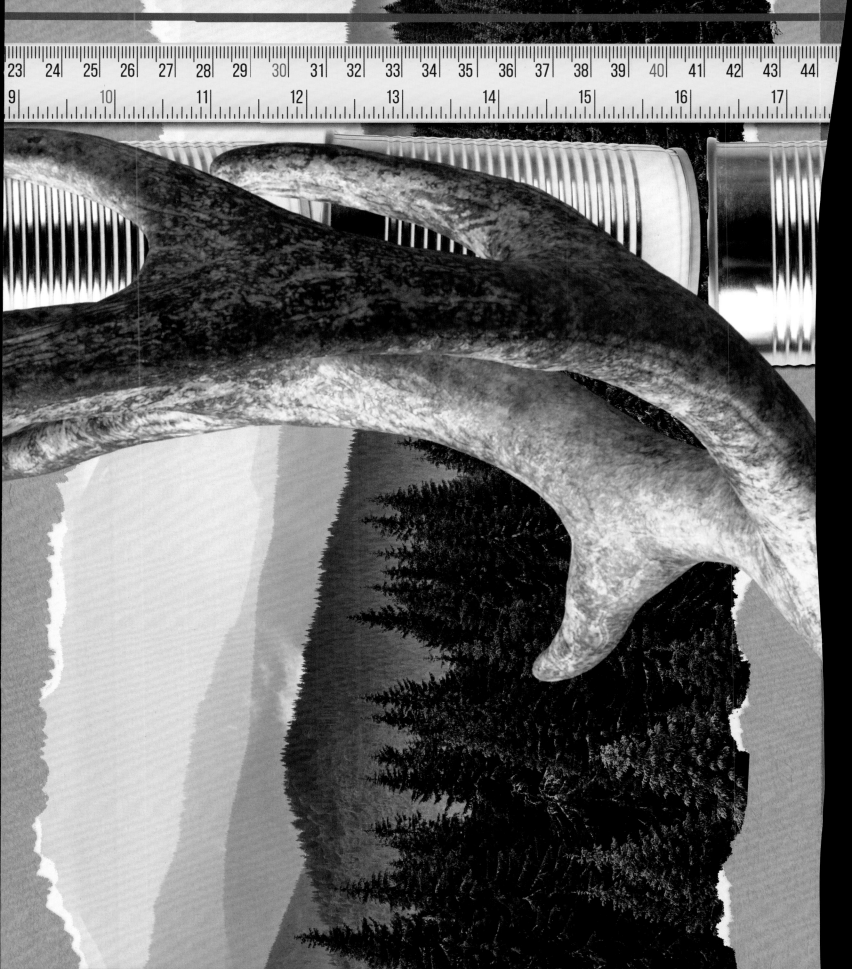

MISSION

FIND OUT WHY CARIBOU ARE ALWAYS MOVING AND NEVER STAY IN ONE PLACE FOR LONG.

CARIBOU ONLY LIVE IN NORTHERN PLACES.

ATTEMPT #1

Hide in the snow until we see the caribou and then follow it to figure out why it never stops moving.

We saw a kid caribou and her mom, but we accidentally scared the kid away. We had to get them back together!

Boy caribou lose their antlers in the fall. Only GIRLS keep their antlers all year round.

But we didn't have to worry. The mom brought her herd to look for her kid. They found her and they sure move fast!

Too fast for us.

Before we could find them again, David's grandpa James came to visit.

And he brought lunch!

While we were at lunch, David and his sister Millie threw away their leftovers.

Then David's grandpa asked his pops why he didn't tell us the stories yet, so we went back to the caribou.

ATTEMPT #2

We saw the caribou mom and kid in the garden looking for food.

They were too fast for us again, so we went back inside.

And Grandpa James told us one of his stories. It was about the caribou and his ancestors, the Dene people. His story made us think that maybe the caribou kept moving because the forest was being cut down.

He told us the caribou and the Dene have always had a special connection.

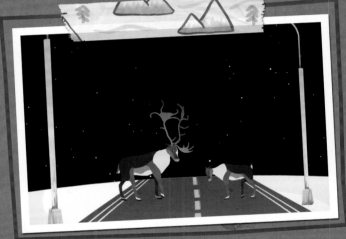

The Dene wanted to make sure their people lived for a long time. So they made a deal with the caribou, to take care of the land and the animals.

But now that more people live near the caribou and are cutting down their forest homes, the caribou need more protection.

Which made us think, that maybe the caribou kept moving because the forests are being cut down.

ATTEMPT #3

So, we used our leftovers as bait to lead the caribou to a safe place with trees and food...

AND IT WORKED!

But they didn't eat everything. They kept moving and we didn't know why.

That's when I remembered something Jane Goodall said:

"How will this decision we're making today affect people in the future?"

-Jane Goodall

When more caribou came, we realized the caribou keep moving because they only take what they need, leaving enough for EVERYONE.

MISSION: COMPLETE ✓

Just like we should do.

TOP 11 FACTS
— CARIBOU —

1

Caribou have SCENT GLANDS on their ankles so, when they sense danger, they go up on their hind legs to release a smell that warns other caribou to stay away.

2

Caribou communicate with each other with SIGHT, SMELL, TOUCH, and SOUND.

PLANT A TREE

ALASKA

YUKON TERRITORY

NORTHWEST TERRITORIES

NUNAVUT

BRITISH COLUMBIA

MANITOBA

3 Caribou make one of the largest animal MIGRATIONS on the planet!

4 CARIBOU CAN LIVE AS FAR NORTH AS THE ARCTIC.

5 A caribou's favorite food is lichen and they dig for it under the snow with their hooves.

6 Caribou hooves are hollowed out and act like a big scoop that they use to DIG for food.

7 The caribou is the only member of the deer family where both boys and girls grow ANTLERS.

recycle

8 CARIBOU LIVE FOR ABOUT FIFTEEN YEARS IN THE WILD.

15

A group of caribou is called a HERD.

9

10 REINDEER AND CARIBOU ARE ACTUALLY THE SAME SPECIES.

11 Caribou like to stick with their HERD and live far away from all other animals.

CARIBOU ONLY

HOW WE CAN HELP

CARIBOU

NAME:

Starr Gauthier

OCCUPATION:

Caribou Guardian

FUN **FACT:**

She also has a really cool first name.

You can start by copying what other people who are already helping CARIBOU are doing.

We're going to copy STARR GAUTHIER.

Which means she's working to help save wild caribou.

That means moving from one place to another.

She told us that some caribou herds migrate because of the temperature and others move to find different types of food.

KLINSE-ZA MATERNITY PEN

Starr works at a MATERNITY PEN.

That means they have a baby inside them.

That's a place where pregnant caribou can safely give birth to their babies.

Called calves.

Once the mom and baby are strong enough, they get released back into the WILD.

More BABIES, more CARIBOU!

165

When Starr was growing up in Saulteau First Nations, there was a program to help local caribou. She **VOLUNTEERED** and now she's hooked on helping make sure caribou don't go extinct.

She also told us that the **BIGGEST THREAT** facing caribou is the loss of the forests they live in.

But forests can GROW BACK, especially if we help them!

PLANT TREES or give to charities
PLANTING TREES where caribou roam.

ASK YOURSELF
DO I REALLY
NEED THIS ?? ??

Also, BUY LESS THINGS. Less things equals less trees and land that needs to be used to make those things.

"We have taken away nature's balances but we can help restore balances."

-Starr Gauche

Help restore balances and save the caribou!

167

TIGER

SCIENTIFIC NAME: PANTHERA TIGRIS

WHERE THEY LIVE

India, Nepal, Bhutan, Bangladesh, Myanmar, Russia, China, Thailand, Malaysia, Indonesia, Cambodia, Laos, and Vietnam

Open here to find out how BIG a tiger's PAW is!

STATUS ⚠️ ⚠️

ENDANGERED

SAVE OUR PLANET

WHAT THEY EAT

I'M A CARNIVORE!

MISSION

There are less than 4000 tigers in the world because people keep taking over their territory.

ATTEMPT #1

Be slow and quiet and find a tiger at night to figure out why they like nighttime best.

We found one and, even though I tried to tell him not to run, Greybeard ran off!

The tiger chased after him!

TIGERS LOVE TO CHASE!

170

Before the tiger got to Greybeard, we got between them.

 But then my mom got between us and our mission.

She said since it was late, I had to get ready for bed. But I said that was the perfect time to finish our mission. She gave us ten more minutes.

ATTEMPT #2

Find the tiger in our apartment building and figure out what it does at night!

The tiger went after Greybeard again and led us right to our neighbor Annisa!

She told us there was an animal living in our apartment building's garden shed. We thought it was a tiger, but it turned out to be another kind of cat.

CATS AND TIGERS ARE IN THE SAME FAMILY.

It was perfect! We could study the cat and learn about the tiger! But the cat didn't seem to want to help. So, we went back to searching for the tiger.

Tigers have really good hearing and can see 6 times better than we can at night.

WHAT WE SEE →

WHAT TIGERS SEE ←

We found the tiger in the laundry room. And guess what? The tiger went after Greybeard again!

I distracted the tiger and then it couldn't find us. BUT my mom did...

and made us all go to bed.

173

We were worried about the tiger until I saw something that made me feel better.

"My mission is to create a world where we can live in harmony with nature."

—Jane Goodall

My mom said sometimes living together peacefully is leaving things alone. Especially wild things.

ATTEMPT #4

The next day, we used Greybeard as tiger bait.

ROARRRRRR!

AND IT WORKED!...SORT OF.

The tiger climbed to get Greybeard and chased him all the way to the roof!

Tigers will sometimes climb to catch their prey.

But we didn't let the tiger get to Greybeard because we scared him away!

That's why the tiger kept going after Greybeard and not us. Tigers don't like humans, and that's why they like the nighttime, because there aren't as many people around.

My mom was right!

MISSION: COMPLETE ✓

TOP 11 FACTS
—TIGER—

① Tigers have existed for <u>millions of years</u>! The first tiger fossils were found in China, and they're two million years old.

② Tigers practice ROARING to make sure their roars are scary.

③ NO TWO TIGERS have the same stripes, just like no two people have the same fingerprints.

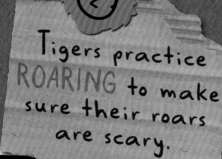

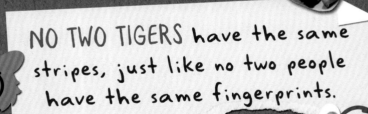

ROARR!

4

Tigers have EYES on the back of their heads. Just kidding! They have white spots on the back of their ears that look like an extra set of eyes and make them look bigger and scarier than they are.

5

GROWN-UP TIGERS CAN EAT A WHOLE GOAT IN ONE SITTING.

6 Tiger pee smells like BUTTERED POPCORN. They use it to mark their territory to keep other tigers away.

7 Baby tigers don't learn to HUNT until they're six months old.

8 IN SHORT BURSTS, TIGERS CAN GO AS FAST AS A CAR!

A group of tigers is called an ambush or a streak.

9

10

Tigers are the BIGGEST wild cats in the world. They weigh as much as 10 of us.

11

TIGERS ARE GOOD SWIMMERS.

HOW WE CAN HELP TIGERS

NAME:
Nayla Azmi

OCCUPATION:
Indigenous Storyteller, Conservationist

Meet other people who are helping TIGERS.

We met NAYLA AZMI.

ROAR

She's working to protect the forests where tigers live!

Indonesia, where Nayla lives, is the only place in the world where ORANGUTANS, RHINOS, ELEPHANTS and TIGERS live together.

NAYLA found a TIGER KITTEN when she was four years old and from then on she's loved tigers.

Nayla started a program to train
FOREST PATROLLERS

Cool name right?

Forest patrollers make sure that forests are SAFE for PLANTS and ANIMALS, but to do that there needs to actually be a forest.

One of the main threats tigers face is LOSS OF HABITAT.

That means the forests they live in are getting cut down.

WHAT CAN WE DO?

STEP 1

Plant trees! Trees help make air for us to breath and give homes to lots of animals.

STEP 2

Plant trees for tigers. Send some money to tiger sanctuaries or groups working to replant forests that have been cut down.

"Be one with the forest. Write down how you feel. Reconnect your soul to the forest, it's our home."
    - Nayla Azmi

Visit a forest near you TODAY!

THANK YOU SOOOOO MUCH for reading my endangered animal guide!

XOXO ♥

I hope it's helped you understand these animals a little bit better.

Because if you UNDERSTAND them, then hopefully you've started to CARE about them.

Because if you care about something, then you probably don't want anything bad to happen to it.

LIKE GOING EXTINCT!!

Please do your part to make sure these animals don't disappear forever. The only way they're going to be saved is if we all work TOGETHER.

Thanks again and remember, if you ever lose hope, (like I do sometimes) look up some HELPFUL QUOTES.

Did I tell you I LOVE quotes? I love them because they're like awesome bits of knowledge that make you think or inspire you to act.

> "It would be absolutely useless for any of us to work to save wildlife without working to educate the next generation of conservationists."
>
> -Jane Goodall

THE GREEN VIBES

We're the NEXT GENERATION OF CONSERVATIONISTS, you and me! So let's start, right now!

Maybe we can even come up with our own quotes. Think about it, what can you say today that might become a helpful quote for someone tomorrow?

See you out in the world, your BEST FRIEND,

Jane

And DAVID!

And Greybeard!

Greybeard asked me to write this, this is his hand print signature

HELPFUL ORGANIZATIONS

There are so many ways you can help all of the animals we've learned about together-check out some of these awesome organizations!

 Jane Goodall Institute
Roots & Shoots

rootsandshoots.global

POLAR BEAR

Polar Bears International

polarbearsinternational.org

GREAT WHITE SHARK

Minorities in Shark Sciences

www.misselasmo.org

Sharks4Kids

www.sharks4kids.com

Bow Seat Ocean Awareness Programs

bowseat.org

HONEY BEE

MoHives   www.mohives.org

ButterBee; formerly Planet   www.butterbee.org/meet-our-hive
Bee Foundation

Planet Bee Foundation   www.planetbee.org

GIANT GOLDEN-CROWNED FLYING FOX

PhilBio (Philippines Biodiversity   www.philbio.org.ph/about-us
Conservation Foundation Inc.)

GHARIAL

World Wildlife Fund India   www.wwfindia.org/about_wwf/
                                             priority_species/threatened_
                                             species/gharial

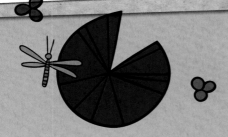
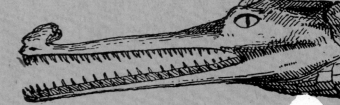

BLUE WHALE

Oceanswell   oceanswell.org

Ocean Conservancy   oceanconservancy.org

MONARCH BUTTERFLY

Save Our Monarchs   www.saveourmonarchs.org

BLACK RHINO

Lewa Wildlife Conservancy   www.lewa.org

Sheldrick Wildlife Trust   www.sheldrickwildlifetrust.org

CARIBOU

Caribou 4 Ever   caribou4ever.ca

TIGER

Nuraga Bhumi Institute   www.nuragabhumi.org/
                              what-we-do

Rainforest Action Network   ran.org

OTHERS

International Union for
Conservation of Nature   www.iucn.org/get-involved

World Wild Fund for
Nature (WWF)   wwf.org

LOVE OUR PLANET

ABOUT THE AUTHORS

My friends J.J. and Christin helped me write my animal guide!

J.J. JOHNSON

J.J. is an multi-Emmy Award winning executive producer and director. He is the creator of Jane and Ghostwriter (AppleTV+), Dino Dana and Annedroids (Amazon Prime Video), Endlings (Hulu) and has built over 30 playgrounds for needy communities with his series Giver (ION TV). J.J. is the coauthor of four books and is an avid dog petter. His favorite animal is the BLUE WHALE.

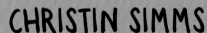

Because there's still so much to learn about them. And because they're the BIGGEST!

CHRISTIN SIMMS

Christin has always loved stories, and storytelling has made her an Emmy Award winning executive producer, a busy TV writer, a newly minted director, and a coauthor of four books. While her favorite animals are dogs, her second favorite are TIGERS.

Mostly because tigers are the world's largest cat. And they have really COOL stripes.

HERE ARE SOME PHOTOS OF US!

DragonFruit, an imprint of Mango Publishing, publishes high-quality children's books to inspire a love of lifelong learning in readers. DragonFruit publishes a variety of titles for kids, including children's picture books, nonfiction series, toddler activity books, pre-K activity books, science and education titles, and ABC books. Beautiful and engaging, our books celebrate diversity, spark curiosity, and capture the imaginations of parents and children alike.

Mango Publishing, established in 2014, publishes an eclectic list of books by diverse authors. We were named the Fastest Growing Independent Publisher by Publishers Weekly in 2019 and 2020. Our success is bolstered by our main goal, which is to publish high quality books that will make a positive impact in people's lives.

Our readers are our most important resource; we value your input, suggestions, and ideas. We'd love to hear from you—after all, we are publishing books for you!

Please stay in touch with us and follow us at:

Instagram: @dragonfruitkids

Facebook: Mango Publishing

Twitter: @MangoPublishing

LinkedIn: Mango Publishing

Pinterest: Mango Publishing

Sign up for our newsletter at www.mangopublishinggroup.com and receive a free book! Join us on Mango's journey to change publishing, one book at a time.